AF447811

PHOENICIAN CIVILIZATION

A BRIEF HISTORY FROM BEGINNING TO END

HISTORY HUB

photo on right: Chris Hartford from London, UK, CC BY 2.0 Wikimedia Commons

Bonus Downloads

*Get Free Books with **Any Purchase** History Shorts*

Every purchase comes with a FREE download!

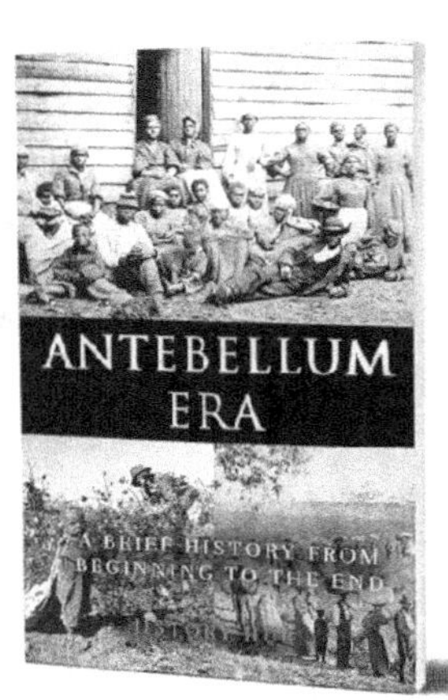

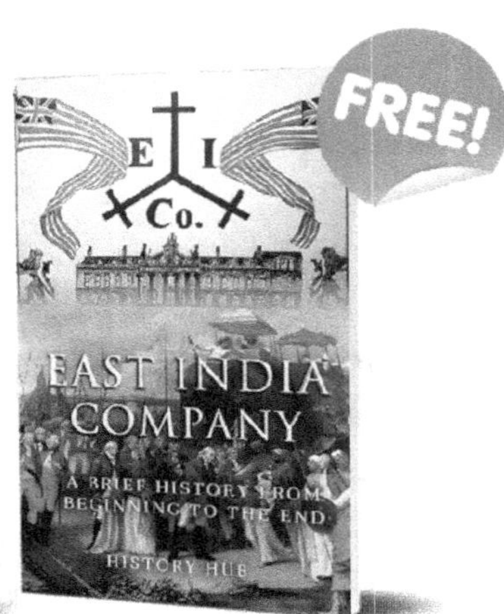

or Click Here.

Phoenician Civilization

A Brief History from Beginning to the End

History Shorts

© 2022 Copyright by History Shorts. All Rights Reserved.

Please Note: The book you are about to enjoy is an analytical review meant for educational and entertainment purposes as an unofficial companion. If you have not yet read the original work, please do before purchasing this copy.

Disclaimer & Terms of Use: No part of this publication may be reproduced or retransmitted, electronic or mechanical, without the written permission of the publisher. The information in this book is meant for educational and entertainment purposes only and the publisher and author make no representations or warranties with respect to the accuracy or completeness of these contents and disclaim all warranties such as warranties of fitness for a particular purpose. Product names, logos, brands, and other trademarks featured or referred to within this publication are the property of their respective trademark holders and are not affiliated with this publication. This is an unofficial summary and analytical review meant for educational and entertainment purposes only and has not been authorized, approved, licensed, or endorsed by the original book's author or publisher and any of their licensees or affiliates.

CONTENTS

Chapter One
Introduction

Cornwall is known to be one of the most holiday destinations in Europe. Its lush green fields and interesting landscape make it a top destination for vacations. Prominent sites like Tintagel Castle which was famous in Arthurian lore as the birthplace of the mythic king revealed early medieval trade links all across Europe and beyond. But during that so-called dark age, this place was once the most important commercial center in the entirety of the North Atlantic.

Three thousand years ago Europe was a very different place, people rode chariots and were mostly pagans. According to archeologists, they were insular groups of people whose information has only come to light in recent decades. The interesting aspect of the information found was that across this route these people seemed united by a similar culture and religious ideas. Not much can be verified due to a complete lack of written sources from this period which will be a recurring factor when it comes to the history of the Phoenician civilization. Cornwall is one of the few places where the remains of the Phoenicians can still be seen today. The famous wild horses of Cornwall are evidence of the Phoenician Empire that existed millennia ago, having originated from the Eurasian side of the world by their breeders and the stone remains that show the buildings of that era.

There isn't much solid evidence besides Cornwall in the modern day that hints at the existence of the Phoenicians. This surprises many as they were the most successful traders in history, often called the first true seafarers of Europe and largely credited for the first true alphabet which was the base of the modern English language. Praised by Homer and Herodotus as expert shipbuilders and referenced in the Bible by the prophet

Ezekiel as "merchants to the people of many coastlines' '; later they were even commandeered by the British Empire. It is believed by some that the Phoenicians can be credited with the building of Soloman's Temple. These tales come off as myths as the real account of the Phoenicians is hampered by a total lack of Phoenician contemporary sources, but the little information that can be found makes them.

The Phoenicians were not like other great ancient civilizations. One of the reasons that getting information from their period is tough is that they did not concentrate much on land acquisitions and conquest so much as they concentrated on commerce and trade. For centuries they ruled the sea trade along the Mediterranean, showing signs of true seamen. According to popular belief, a seaman must be someone that can anticipate where the weather is going, know how to navigate in the roughest weather and calm waters, and be of a strong constitution to withstand the rocky waters and not get seasick.

As they were the first to adopt this method of trade it kept them in a position of power for centuries. They had emerged after the collapse of many civilizations that had left many civilizations starting from zero. This period would be known as the Phoenician Renaissance by some and perhaps is the origin of the myth of the Phoenix where it rises from the ashes after burning in fire.

Chapter Two
The Origin - The Modern Rediscovery of the Phoenician Empire

The cities of southern Spain have a rich history like Marbella, Cartagena, Algecrica, Malaga, and other ports where Romans, vandals, Visigoths, burglars, Arabs, and Castilians all left their mark. However, most people don't realize that the founding predates all those civilizations. It seems that the ones that built Spain's cities originated from elsewhere. In the early 1960s, archeologists discovered the vestiges of an ancient cemetery near the resort town of Almunecar which was a Phoenician colony of Sexi. They initially thought that they had escalated the remains of early Greek colonists in the region; however, it soon became clear that the ceramics being uncovered were from even further East than Greece. The design was similar to those found in the Iron- age world of the Middle East especially in the region during biblical times such as Canaan.

In the decades that followed several sites with similar artifacts were discovered not only in Spain, but in Morocco, Malta, Sardinia, Sicily, and even as far away as Britain. The archeologists concluded that these discoveries were a sign of a civilization that had settled en masse throughout the Mediterranean. The biggest problem with their discovery was that there is no recorded history of a Phoenician calling themselves a Phoenician or referring to themselves as a collective term. In their inscriptions which are scarce, they describe themselves according to their families and cities. Not in terms of a common culture. Phoenician archaeology speaks to that as well as their cities often adapted to the cultures near them. The city of Byblos looked more to Egypt than its neighbors. Sidon looked more to Persia whilst Tyre had close links to Judea and Jerusalem.

As stated before, there is little written text from Phoenicians that can explain their society. Outside sources that wrote about the Phoenicians civilization though, almost unanimously despised everything they were. Some historians wonder "what would we know of Greece and Rome if all accounts of them had been burned and destroyed aside from those written by their enemies" Thus telling the history of the Phoenicians is a detective story. A French Scholar called Ernest Renan (1823-1892) took part in the first wide-scale excavations of the runs in Ashkelon.

History would reveal that the Phoenician people were a hard people to understand. They did not refer to themselves as Phoenicians and rarely thought of themselves as a unit. The independent city-states that formed the Phoenician empire . The Phoenicians themselves did not have a name for themselves but identified more with the city-states that they were born into. This would possibly be the reason for the downfall of the

Phoenicians. Historically a strong sense of identity and unity is what would keep a society at the top of history. In fact, it is through the study of genetics that scientists were able to discern that the ancient skeletons that they found along the shores of the Mediterranean were intrinsically linked and showed that they were all part of the same colony.

Considering the vast amount of power that the Phoenicians held at some point, it's baffling to realize that proof of their existence was almost completely wiped out. Being seafaring traders, history shows that their main focus was on profiteering. Initially, they room over territory and cities to gain access to more resources for trade in a way that was unique to the time. Through the benefits that trade with them had on the economy they managed to take over large amounts of land eventually colonizing most of the Mediterranean. That system worked well for them. Other cities along the Mediterranean could not travel as freely as them and at times were resource dry. Due to banditry and harsh conditions, it was easy for cities to fall into poverty and poverty. There isn't much record of those times, but archeologists have used biblical references to figure out that famine could lead to devastation so severe that people would resort to cannibalism, trading the rule of their city to get food was a good deal to many struggling independent cities along the Mediterranean. Against the independent cities, the Phoenicians had superior military power through sheer resources, but they were not an aggressive group in general.

There is still significant information lost about the Phoenicians that archeologists have attributed to their weird method of colonization and weak military power. When they conquered territories, they did not impose their values and laws on the people. They tended to merge with the communities and their cultures fused naturally unlike the domineering personalities of the Roman empire that would dominate the seas after the Phoenicians.

Chapter Three
The Origin - How Phoenician Civilization Began and Was Organized

The story of the Phoenicians begins far before the Iron Age. Their entire society geared itself toward the sea. Just like other ancient seafaring people and being the first, the sea was a highway. That form of transport was easier to navigate than the land that surrounded them. As long as they paid homage to larger societies such as Egypt to keep the peace, they were left to their own devices. The Phoenician civilization is believed to have begun around 1500 B.C having descended from Canaanite society. They had a language and practiced a similar religion to their ancestors.

Like Canaan, Phoenicia was never a unified kingdom with a federation of relatively independent city-states each with its own ruler. The most famous of whom were Hiram(King Of Tyre 980-947 B.C), Pygmalion (King of Tyre 831-785 BC) or Ahiram (King of Byblos). There is no information at all about who the rulers of Sidon were. They worshiped gods such as Baal and Resheph. According to some, the Phoenicians also made human sacrifices. When it came to politics though, each society went its own way. Though several Bronze Age eras societies coveted Canaan, only the Egyptians would have a lay of the Canaanite land that would eventually become Phoenicia. However, Egypt's power would end in the 12 century BC. Groups of migrants and marauders known as the sea people showed up along the shores of the empires of the Eastern Mediterranean. Modern historians don't know what happened or why they left their homes, but one thing is clear is that that part of the world after their arrival would never be the same. According to Egyptian, Lugaritic, Cypriot and other texts, the arrival of the sea people led to the collapse of the Late Bronze Age Collapse of the 12th century BC.

These violent series of events brought about the complete destruction of the Hittite Empire (1600-1178 BC) as well as Egyptian domination in Canaan. When the dust of the turmoil had settled, several new societies sprouted including the Phoenician city states independent of Egyptian rule. Surprisingly the Phoenician city states were left largely unscathed by the sea peoples leading historians to believe that they had colluded with the invaders. With the absence of Egyptian rule, the city states of Byblos, Sidon and Tyre started to grow economically. This was a testament to the adaptability of these city-states.

In the years 1200-1000 BC Phoenician alphabet spawned, likely inspired by Canaanite writing systems. In Byblos, five royal inscriptions denote this time on the Ahiram sarcophagus showing the existence of the Phoenician twenty-two letter alphabet. Another important structure of this time is the Temple of the Obelisks where Egyptian hieroglyphics give way to the Phoenician alphabet. It's suspected that it was easier for merchants to keep records and contact trade partners. Phoenician ports became trade hubs for all sorts of goods. The most sought-after of their goods were cedar trees and timber for building ships. Their biggest customers were Egypt which had almost no forests to garner wood from. This trade would continue for thousands of years to come. They also traded in manufactured goods crafted from stone, precious metals, wood, wool and even ivory from south of the Sahara. Such things were traded at numerous overseas destinations by the seafaring merchants who in return brought gold, silver, and spices from lands away.

They managed to expand their power by becoming middlemen for trade between cities. Phoenician artisans were also known to take raw materials from other countries and turn them into finished goods, selling them around the world. This wasn't the only way they gained power, they also expanded into other areas. Areas that were rich in natural resources. Areas that no one else in the East had access to. The Phoenician civilization at that point did not have the manpower or resources for war to take over other people's land, so they took to the seas. Over centuries that is what would set up their colonies. The most famous of these colonies would be Carthage (in present-day Tunisia).

Though ancient writers believe that these colonies were founded in the 12th century BC, modern scholars estimate a more recent date such as 900 or 800 BC. Smaller waystations existed for the Phoenicians before the establishment of permanent cities that allowed them to build their wealth in trade before setting up permanent settlements. But others would go on to become immense commercial and military powers surpassing the cities from which they came.

Chapter Four
The Origin - How the Phoenicians Established Themselves

The Phoenicians could be considered the first capitalists. Being motivated by the profit they took on the risks of carrying cargo by sea. Other civilizations before had hesitated to sail out of the sight of land or during the night, this meant little to the Phoenicians, using the landmarks, the stars, and eventually nautical instruments, they navigated the seas. Making ports wherever they went, Phoenicians would leave their mark on the desperate people that they would chance upon. Finding desperate communities was not unusual and it is estimated that every thirty miles or so along the Mediterranean a Phoenician colony seemed to have sprouted up. These would be waystations for ambitious merchants to make their fortune. Notably, Cadiz in Spain was an established mercantile center. It's even thought that these Phoenician newcomers began to influence the Celtic and Iberian people of the peninsula. Widespread colonization took place, not just commercial activity. In all likelihood, particularly in Sardinia, wars were fought between independent leaders and incoming merchant powers. Perhaps supported by swords for hire as Carthage later was. THese wars were left completely unrecorded in surviving histories and can only be deduced by archeologists studying the ancient architecture and bones along the Mediterranean. Although initially motivated by profit, they may have suffered drought and famine forcing them to look for greener pastures. The first area believed to have been colonized by Phoenician traders as early as the 11century BC was the nearby island of Cyprus. Cyprus was replete with valuable minerals and copper. The largest Phoenican community was based in Kition which started as a small trading outpost and grew into a prosperous city. After some time Kition would also contain a large Greek population.

The Phoenicians along with the Aegeans established sizable settlements in Italy. Over here though, they had to fight for dominance with Greek colonizers. Their activities were constrained to the northwest because of this because it was a much safer place for them because of its proximity to Phoenician settlements in North Africa. It would protect them from Greek attacks. Some of the furthest settlements were in Spain and what is now France and Britain's unfortunately evidence of these colonies are yet to be found but through archeological research and deductions there's a very high chance that they were well-established. Here, Phoenicians conducted trade with the locals offering items such as glass, oil and ceramics in return for silver and tin. This wasn't the only place Phoenician settlers went to. Some historians claim that Phoenicians went all the way to the south of the Sahara. It is in Africa that the most visible of those remnants can be seen. The greatest being Carthage. Carthage was thought to have been colonized by Tyre. Due to less local inhabitants and an abundance of resources the Phoenicians would have been encouraged to establish permanent residence. This allowed for rapid growth and a power growing to the point that it was rivaling Rome. Rome would learn much from their seafaring ways, conduct and how to conduct war and take over territory, how to build commercial ties and military strategy. It is suspected that the Phoenicians went as far as Sub-saharan Africa and traded at a trade center that would later be known as Great Zimbabwe. The irony of two lost ancient societies revealing details about each other has not escaped the notice of historians. Although traditionally the building of Great Zimbabwe was credited to the Phoenicians to make clear through its unique architecture and conduct that this was a trade city established by the local Bantu tribe that had established itself there. It is suspected that the Phoenicians realized that they could not colonize that part of the world due to not having enough military power and it was more profitable to conduct peaceful trade there.

Scientists have also been key in understanding how the Phoenicians established themselves. Through analyzing ancient DNA and conducting tests they have been able to understand how the Phoenicians integrated with the members of the communities there. Genetics play a large part in this as the traditional Phoenicans would have descended from the Middle East, those Phoenicians that lived in Carthage genetic makeup would show whether the Phoenicians reproduced with Carthegeon women and that would be matched to the infrastructure and remnants that could be found. That would tell how Phoenicians affected the culture from the infrastructure to the burials and the genetics. Any mutations in the DNA were conducted by scientists were largely attributed to not only intermarrying but also genetics changing through exposure to weather and living conditions that their forefathers did not experience which is testament to the fact that Phoenicians traveled to look for greener pastures.

Chapter Five

The Rise - Trade, Production and Commerce

Having been sandwiched by the Hittites and the Jewish states for a while, when the sea peoples ravished the Mediterranean breaking down Egypt's dominion over that part of the world. Since the Phoenicians didn't view themselves as a cohesive community, but as city states it allowed them to have a fluidity and adaptability (much like the water). Despite being separate they were united and had similar ways of conducting themselves. They all turned their backs to the tough mountains that contained indomitable enemies that forced them to turn to the sea. The term Phoenician is confusing because the origin of the meaning is unclear, but it is widely believed that the term came from the Greek meaning the color purple. The purple would be their trademark eventually but before that the Phoenicians could be described as the first capitalists. Being concentrated in the Middle East they learned that their environment wasn't conducive for growth unless they were able to somehow get ahold of the resources of other territories. The only resource that they were really rich in was Cedar wood.

The cedar wood would be vital to building their ships that would open up the Mediterranean to them. The reason that the Phoenicians turned to the sea was because the terrain that they initially abided in was hostile and not just conducive for trade. The roads aside from having rough terrain also were infested with bandits. The Phoenicians were known to be very calculating and took cost-benefit analysis into consideration.

Facing the sea was scary, but the right ship's configuration posed a lower risk than finding a way to face the roads.

Before the Phoenicians seafarers, there was no other civilization that dared to venture out to the sea in the evening or where they could not see the shore. This allowed them to dominate quickly in trade as they used innovation to create ships, initially called the bireme. The bireme had two banks of oars that could travel long distances without succumbing to the harsh conditions of the sea. The seafarers started trading materials between ports until they realized that it was more profitable to establish ports in the areas that they traded in. Trading via sea was a groundbreaking invention during that era. The exact dates were hard to determine due to the Phoenician records being almost destroyed.

Their bravery to face the seas allowed them to grow exponentially, especially after many of the societies were ravaged by the sea peoples (an unidentifiable group of people that caused havoc in the Middle East effectively ending Egypt's dominance during the Bronze Age. It's unclear where they came from or what their purpose was. There is speculation that since they left the Phoenicians largely unscathed that there was an agreement between them that stopped the sea peoples from ravaging the Phoenicians.) The combination of widespread poverty started by the sea people and the innovation of the Phoenicians made them a force to be reckoned with quite quickly. Their position as desired traders strengthened as they learned to forge different things using resources from multiple areas. Their position as the greatest traders in the Mediterranean would only improve when they discovered how to make purple.

Chapter Six
The Rise - Purple Dye

The color purple would be the cusp of Phoenician existence when they discovered that they could obtain the color purple (currently known as Tyrian Purple). The color purple would become one of the focal points of Phoenician trade. They obtained the color purple from Murex snails which are known to be a predatory snail that secreted purple when it attacked. They would collect the dye by poking the snails in order to obtain the purple secretion. The less labor-intensive way of obtaining the dye was by crushing them. Before then there was no way to obtain purple dye. The process was difficult and required many snails in order to obtain it. Having enough for an entire gown or robe would cost a fortune which is why purple became a royal color. The Tyrian Purple was of the highest quality because its color did not easily fade but became brighter with exposure to sunlight. For just one gram of Tyrian purple, they had to crush about ten thousand Murex snails.

Only people of the highest social standing were allowed to wear purple and how much purple you could wear depended on your rank. The popularity of purple among the royals and nobles is shown by the mountain of discarded shells at Sidon in modern-day Lebanon that has created a mountain 40 meters high. The Phoenician trade empire began to thrive on the color purple. The value was considered greater than its weight in gold and silver.The Phoenicians used this to their advantage using their proceeds to build powerful ships from cedarwood. With the proceeds from purple, they could be innovative with the construction of their boats.

During the height of the sale of purple they invented the boat, trireme. Trireme means three rower which was the development of the penteconter(a previous ship model that had been used). Each oar was manned by one man. These ships were often used for sea warfare which put the Phoenicians at an advantage against anyone that tried to challenge them at sea. With the sale of Tyrian purple and the trireme the Phoenicians started to travel beyond the sight of land which is what led to the establishment of their port towns.

Tyrian Purple would be what would make the city of Tyre the powerhouse of the Phoenician empire. Using this economic advantage over their surrounding areas they were able to colonize the surrounding areas. The wealth that Tyre gained through the sale of Tyrian purple was safe for many centuries because the city was hard to reach. It would require an enemy that could match The Phoenician wealth and an enemy that was wily enough to get to the very isolated island. Up until that point, only the Phoenicians had the ability to navigate the seas proficiently and safely travel large distances without too much damage. The disadvantage that those who wanted to face the Phoenicians faced as well was that if they tried to reach them via

boat it gave the Phoenicians time to spot them and send a
barrage of arrows their way, sinking their ships. It wouldn't be
until Alexander the Great that the great city of Tyre would fall
and lose her riches.

Chapter Seven
The Rise - Carthage

Today Carthage tends to only be remembered in relation to its destruction through Roman conquest. The memory of Carthage was left to the ashes, but it was probably one of the epitomes of Phoenician society. By mastering ocean navigation and trade with the sale of purple, Phoenicians could expand their efforts. Fueling their hunger for growth, the Phoenicians realized that competing with other dominant societies for colonies wasn't lucrative enough. At that point Tyre was the most powerful and lucrative of the Phoenician cities. Myth says that Dydo was running away from Pygmalian, her brother, who had murdered her husband (her husband was the high priest of Tyre). She escaped to North Africa with colonialists and other resources. She was known to be a very wily and smart woman. She used trickery to establish herself there. She was told that she could keep her people in the area on the map that a cow hide could cover. She cleverly cut the cow hide into strips and seized an area big enough to cover a city. She named the place Qart-Hadarsht which was Phoenician for "New City". Thus, Carthage was born.

It started as a small trade settlement that was initially at the mercy of their neighbors, paying rent to use the land. According to legend Dydo killed herself because there was pressure for her to marry one of the local chiefs. The rise of Carthage would come from the downfall of Tyre. The Siege of Tyre (585-573 BC) by the Babylonians would leave Tyre weaker and unable to manage the affairs of Carthage. The power vacuum that was left by Tyre in the Mediterranean was replaced by Carthage. Carthage first began its rise locally by the 5th Century BC, they liberated themselves from the indentured servitude of the native Libyans, establishing themselves as settlers. Then they moved on to become the leading regional power with great influence over Utica, Hippocras and the other Phoenician settlements of North Africa. From there, Carthage began to look to dominating cities across the Mediterranean intent on claiming the throne of ports that Tyre had once held. Tyre had dominated its colonies almost solely through economic pressure, Carthage would be the one that would on record use military force to take over. Carthage's navy was formidable and feared by the surrounding societies and their army would see deployment in foreign lands. Carthage established a new model of hegemony which stepped away from the more relaxed Phoenican model and took on the characteristics of a more traditional empire.

As Carthage's sphere of influence grew, so did her cultural dominance. Local groups were being absorbed into its cities and territories while the Punic language spread as the primary Phoenician dialect across the empire. But this system was still not one of complete domination. Compared to most other historical empires it was actually very hands-off. Only the immediate hinterlands to the city were governed by the Cartheginians, while the rest to the empire was controlled through means of treaties. They would pay tributes to Carthage and have diplomatic relations. The cities under Carthage pretty much retained full control. This new empire was not afraid to flex its muscles and this new empire's growth was fast and forceful.

Are You Enjoying Reading?

As an independent publisher

with a tiny marketing budget

we rely on readers, like you.

If you're receiving help from this book,

would you please take a moment to write a brief review?

We really appreciate it.

Chapter Eight
The Fall of Tyre

The beginning of the end of Phoenicia was signified by the end of fall of Tyre. Tyre was the first major Phoenician city of note that controlled multiple colonies. It grew because of the fame of Tyrian purple and their ability to create ships from cedar wood that could manage in waters that other societies would not brave. They are the ones that would establish the Phoenician people as great seafarers. While they were able to venture out and overcome independent rulers to establish colonies and settlements, they often had to flee when faced with real military threats. Such was the case in Italy and in other places along the Mediterranean which made it difficult for them to take over large amounts of land. At first, they were able to survive and build colonies through economic control. The Phoenicians were able to transport goods along long distances more efficiently than the merchants on land. But military power was eventually needed.

Due to much of Phoenician history being lost, there is very little detail of what happened during the siege except what is recorded in the Bible. In approximately 586–573 BC for thirteen years Tyre was at war with the Neo-Babylonian King Nebuchadnezzar. It was prophesied in the Bible that Tyre would fall. According to the book *Commentary on Ezekiel,* it is believed that King Nebuchadnezzar could not attack Tyre using conventional methods because it was an island city. A geographic advantage had saved them from many wars before. King Nebuchadnezzar had to be creative in conquering the city.The Neo-Babylonian soldiers used boulders to build a causeway that led to Tyre. The war between Tyre and Babylonia would result in Tyre being depleted of a lot of resources. It would also serve as a blueprint later on when Alexander the Great would take over the city.

War with King Nebuchadnezzar left the Phoenician city weak. They had control over much of the Mediterranean and their dialect was the most widely spoken at the time. The war proved to their enemies how vulnerable the Phoenician city-states could be against an actual threat. Logically why would the colonies and trading partners of the Phoenicians continue to trade with them when they could conquer them and take over their trade routes and make them their slaves that they could force to build them ships?

In 332 BC Alexander the Great was able to use his military genius to overcome Tyre. It was already weakened from losing its grip on its war with Babylonia. From there on Carthage had taken up much of its former glory. That does not detract from Alexander The Great's victory against The island city. Control over Tyre meant control over the Mediterranean Sea. Using material from the ancient ruins of The old Tyre to build a walkway to the island. The feat was no small one. Eventually, the people of Tyre noticed that Alexander the Great was trying to conquer their city. They tried everything to destroy and discourage their forces. But Alexander was relentless. It took seven months for Alexander to conquer Tyre. When the men of Tyre noticed that the battle might turn bad, they sent their women and children to Carthage. They would stay and protect the city. That decision would cost them their lives as Alexander would conquer the city and pillage it ruthlessly.

Chapter Nine
The Fall of Carthage (The Punic Wars)

The fall of Carthage would be what the once powerful empire would be known for down in history. It is known that the fall of Tyre was the prosperity of Carthage. The first punic war was when the Roman Empire was rapidly expanding. Carthage was different from Tyre because they were much more militant. They didn't just rely on economic power to consolidate their position. A lesson learned from Tyre. During 480 BC Rome and Carthage were the powers of the West Mediterranean. Initially, their trade relations were good, and Carthage even provided Romans with materials and resources that the Romans used to build their ships and eventually weapons. Carthage supported Rome during its Pyrrhic Wars with materials to build weapons with.

The first Punic War would be to attain dominion of Sicily which at the time (264 BC) was a Carthaginian colony. It ended with the Romans being the victors but both sides of the war lost many men and resources. In 218 BC Hannibal(a Carthaginian general) would spark the second Punic War in an attempt to take over the Roman cities. The territories he targeted were largely in Spain and Italy. The Roman general, Fabius Maximus Cunctator harassed Hannibal without actually engaging him in battle which resulted in some heavy Roman losses. These losses caused the Roman Empire to unite against Hannibal which won them the Battle of Zama in 202 BC.

The Third Punic War (149–146 BC) would be where the great Carthage would finally fall. This war would be fought completely in Carthage in what is considered modern day Northern Tunisia. In 149, the Roman Army would land hostilely in Utica. The Carthaginians thought that they would be able to avoid a war with the Romans if they gave up their weapons and tried to negotiate peace. That was not a wise decision, the Romans besieged the city and now had easier access to Carthage. Even though besieging Utica had been easy, the way to Carthage did not come without struggle. The Roman army started to progress more smoothly when General Scipio took over. He made sure that he blocked supplies from reaching Carthage. Carthage tried to rally its resources but did not efficiently enough to thwart its opponent. In 146 BC The Roman army managed to raid and destroy Carthage showing no mercy. The Roman army had the support of surrounding cities that wished for a Carthage by conceding power to Rome. The Romans pillaged the city for days killing men, women, and children. They only took hostages during the last day of their raid. The once prosperous city had fallen hard at the hands of Roman invaders. They left 50,000 people as slaves who were shipped off and sold to many different cities. Carthage became part of The

Roman Empire and Utica was proclaimed its capital. Perhaps it was because Utica had shown no resistance to their invasion.

The fall of Carthage would be so fast and shocking that one would think it had never had military power. They had fought Rome before, but perhaps the young General Scipio was much too skilled for the Carthaginian army to win against. The end of Carthage marked the end of Phoenicia. Rome would attempt to destroy all signs Phoenicia had ever existed. And they nearly succeeded.

Chapter Ten
Aftermath - The Roman Empire

The Roman Empire conquering Carthage meant that the sea was now controlled by the Romans. After the Punic Carthage was destroyed it took more than a century for a new city to be erected. The Roman city of Carthage by the third century BC would be one of the biggest cities that was part of the Roman Empire and was one of the centers along with Utica of Roman-run North Africa. The city grew to a population of more than 100,000 people. Which is significantly less than the population of Punic Carthage. The city grew due to Julius Caesar's investment into it. Rome's power over North Africa was broken when it fell out of favor with Lucius Domitius Alexander after a Roman consul wanted him to send his son to Rome as a hostage to prove his loyalty to Rome. Alexander had no such loyalty and declared himself emperor of North Africa with the support of his army. Carthage became the capital of the Northern African provinces and as far as Sardinia. Alexander was already an advanced age at the time of his ascension. The Romans rallied their troops to quell the Alexandrian rebellion. They recaptured the lands that Alexander had seized and took Alexander as a prisoner. The exact year that they overthrew Alexander is not known but is suspected to have been between 309 BC to 311 BC. Alexander was sentenced to death and strangled for his insurrection.

The Germanic tribe called Vandals would take over Carthage. Initially, it is suspected that the Vandals were searching for safety in 429 BC. They would eventually clash with the Roman settlements and take over Carthage and other Roman colonies in Africa by 435 BC. The ruler of the Vandals, King Gaiseric was accepted easily by the population of the city particularly because Catholic Christians did not like him. During their conquest of Vandal, it can be concluded that many Roman buildings and churches were destroyed during the Vandal takeover. The Roman Empire was determined to regain their territories again. The first two attempts in the 5th century by Marjorian and Basiliscus to recapture the cities failed. The Vandals were subdued in The Vandalic War (533-534 BC) by the Roman general Belisarius. He chose not to massacre the city, sparing the lives of many people. Carthage at that point became the seat of the praetorian prefecture of Africa for the Roman Empire. There would be wars and disputes among the Roman rulers about who would have control over the city.

Even Roman control would fall to Islamic expansion from Egypt in 647. The initial expansion fell a bit flat. But in 670 to 683. From there, there was a power tug-of-war between the Muslims and the Byzantines. Its last Muslim conquerors in 698 were afraid that East Roman Empire would reclaim Carthage. So they destroyed the city walls, the water supply was cut off, and the agricultural land was pillaged thus ending the reign of the Romans in the second century.

Despite it being destroyed once again, archeologists have uncovered evidence that people continued to use it as a trade center and abided there for hundreds of years.

Chapter Eleven
Conclusion

The Phoenicians were pioneers of their time, engineering their way into the new world by creating a new way of transporting much-needed goods and services. Their ability to adapt and garner resources is a testament to how scholarly their society was. Being the civilization that would be the blueprint for communication and business until the present day one can only think that there is so much valuable information lost from them that we can barely fathom. Even with the vestiges of information that historians have slaved to dig up, one can't help but wonder what more the ancient civilization had achieved.

The scarce information about the Phoenicians also reveals a major fact about dominant societies. That history can only truly be written in the words of the victor. Almost all information that is available about Phoenician society is derived from non-Phoenician sources that inevitably wrote about them in a bad light. Having had their infrastructure and society pillaged, burned, and destroyed by the Romans. That there is anything left is a miracle in itself, but also a lesson that a society could not grow great without military power. For centuries Phoenicians had managed to live in relative peace through their dominion of the seas until the Romans created their seafaring empire and wanted to bump them to the side. The Romans developed ships coupled with their militant army and crushed the Phoenician cities with places such as Carthage being decimated with barely a resistance.

Inevitably as tragic as the story of Phoenician society is, it is a testament to the fact that the contributions and achievements of a society can never truly be destroyed. Regardless of the Roman effort, Phoenicia is still the beginning of the alphabet that we use today and is credited with the development of the ancient world through trade. And above all perhaps...we wouldn't have the color purple if it wasn't for the creative and capitalist pursuits of history's first seafarers.

Chapter Twelve

Discussion Question

Considering the fact that people get facts wrong about current civilizations still existing, how accurate is the information about Phoenicians? In the end is it little more than a fairytale or are archeologists and anthropologists trustworthy in gathering information?

Discussion Question

Colonization is a recurring topic in many civilizations that managed to gain power in the past. In current times it's viewed as a gross human injustice. In your opinion, would the world have developed as it had if colonization had not happened, especially since the Phoenician civilization is the origins of modern sea trade which has made many other civilizations develop?

Discussion Question

Should Carthage have helped Tyre recover from its war with King Nebuchadnezzar? Would that have changed the course of history if Tyre had managed to maintain its power?

Discussion Question

Carthage was much more militant than Tyre. Considering that military power through history was needed to maintain power, what do you think was the weakness in the Carthginian military that led to its downfall.

Discussion Question

Phoenicia managed to gain some colonies through economic advantage. How do you think that was possible? Could poverty have contributed to it?

Discussion Question

What do you believe was the reason that Rome tried to wipe out Phoenician society? Was it simply a need to conquer or were they desperate to take control of the seas and Mediterranean?

Discussion Question

Could Phoenicia be considered a civilization when they were independent city-states? Could Carthage and Tyre really be considered part of the same country when they had strained relations?

Discussion Question

Tyrian purple was what would make Tyre prosperous. But the process of extracting it from snails was arduous and workers who did that were smelly due to the stench of the snails. Jewish women were legally allowed to divorce their husband if he worked with Murex snails. We're the social and environmental consequences worth the development of Tyre?

Chapter Thirteen
Quiz Question

1. **True/False:**The Phoenicians developed open-sea navigation. This skill is what allowed them to develop their society despite not concentrating on acquiring land and conquests.

2. **True or False.** The Phoenicians invented the original alphabet that modern English is based on. Ironically there are very few texts that survive from the Phoenician era.

3. **True/False:**Byblos is one of the only remains of ancient Phoenician civilization that managed to survive. It is in what is considered Lebanon now. Byblos is ranked as one of the 20 world's oldest cities.

4. **True/False:**Rome and Spain joined together to conquer Carthage. Carthage was a strong military power. Spain took some of Carthage's colonies.

5. **True/False:**There is extensive evidence and literature that confirms the existence of the Phoenician civilization. It has helped archeologists figure out how the society operated.

6. **True/ False:**The Phoenicians invented the color purple. It was such an expensive and difficult color to make that purple was a sign of extreme wealth that often only royals could wear. Even in the modern day, the color purple means wealth and royalty.

7. **True/False:**The name for Phoenicia is believed to have come from the Romans. It described the purple dye they obtained from Murex snails that they would become famous for.

8. **True/False:**Pythagoras (who invented the Pythagorean Theorem) was born to a Phoenician father. It is suspected that many great scholars came of Phoenician descent and that Phoenician civilization was very scholarly.

Quiz Answer

1. True

2. True

3. True

4. False, Rome conquered Carthage alone.

5. False, there is very little evidence of the Phoenician civilization and archeologists have struggled to get details about it's existence.

6. . True

7. False, it's believed the name came from Greek.

8. True

Bibliography (Works Cited)

1. "Are they your ancient ancestors?" "Tiktok"
   <https://vm.tiktok.com/ZMFjgV1Fe/>

2. "The Phoenician Civilization" "Apple Podcasts"
   <https://podcasts.apple.com/za/podcast/everything-everywhere-daily/id1521870190?i=1000569123316>

3. "The Entire History of the Phoenicians" "YouTube"
   <https://youtu.be/-p8OZz5KJoo>

4. "Sea Peoples", " Wikipedia"
   <https://en.m.wikipedia.org/wiki/Sea_Peoples>

5. "Roman Carthage" "Wikipedia"
   <https://en.m.wikipedia.org/wiki/Roman_Carthage>

6. "Third Punic War", "Wikipedia"
   <https://en.m.wikipedia.org/wiki/Third_Punic_War>

7. "Punic Wars", "Britannica"
   <https://www.britannica.com/facts/Punic-Wars>

8. "The Siege Tyre", "Wikipedia"
   <https://en.m.wikipedia.org/wiki/Siege_of_Tyre_(586–573_BC)>

9. "First Punic War", "Wikipedia"
   <https://en.m.wikipedia.org/wiki/Punic_Wars>

10. "A History of the Color Purple", "Art and Collections" <https://www.artsandcollections.com/a-history-of-the-colour-purple/>

Images

1. Part 4, Ancient Rome + <"Ancient Rome" by Miguel Virkkunen Carvalho is licensed under CC BY 2.0. To view a copy of this license, visit https://creativecommons.org/licenses/by/2.0/?ref=openverse.>

2. Part 1, Remnants of Phoenicia + <"Paestum# 28 - Cerere's Temple" by Chiara Marra is licensed under CC BY 2.0. To view a copy of this license, visit https://creativecommons.org/licenses/by/2.0/?ref=openverse.>

3. Part 2 Carthage, Cisterns at Carthage + <"Tunisia-3063 - Cisterns at Carthage" by archer10 (Dennis) is licensed under CC BY-SA 2.0. To view a copy of this license, visit https://creativecommons.org/licenses/by-sa/2.0/?ref=openverse.>

4. Part 2 Purple Dye, Murex Snail + <"Bolinus cornutus (horned murex snail) 1" by James St. John is licensed under CC BY 2.0. To view a copy of this license, visit https://creativecommons.org/licenses/by/2.0/?ref=openverse.>

5. Part 1, Phoencian Ship Building + <"Bolinus cornutus (horned murex snail) 1" by James St. John is licensed under CC BY 2.0. To view a copy of this license, visit https://creativecommons.org/licenses/by/2.0/?ref=openverse.>

6. **Part 1, Phoenician Colonies + <"File:Griechischen und phönizischen Kolonien.jpg" by Gepgepgep is licensed under CC BY-SA 3.0. To view a copy of this license, visit https://creativecommons.org/licenses/by-sa/3.0?ref=openverse.>**

Bonus Downloads

*Get Free Books with **Any Purchase** History Shorts*

Every purchase comes with a FREE download!

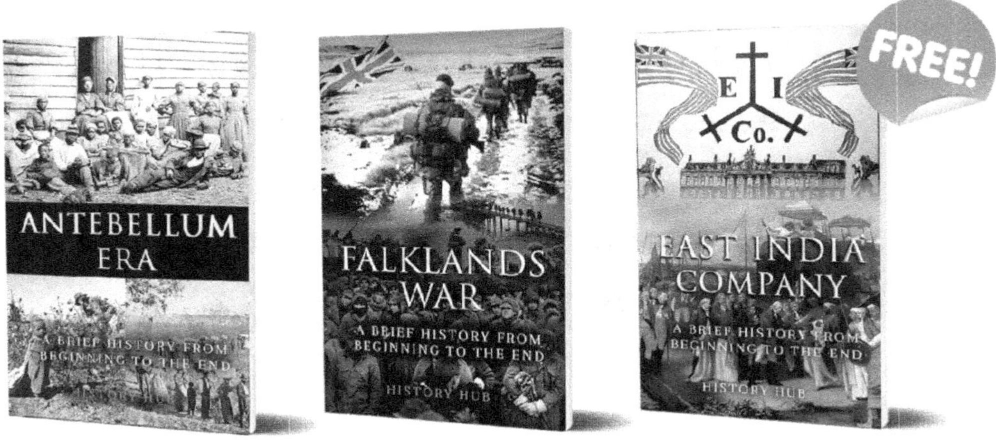

<u>or Click Here.</u>

Thank You For Reading

As an independent publisher

with a tiny marketing budget

we rely on readers, like you.

If you're receiving help from this book,

would you please take a moment to write a brief review?

We really appreciate it.

www.ingramcontent.com/pod-product-compliance
Lightning Source LLC
Chambersburg PA
CBHW080848160726
47999CB00009B/3038